A Note to Parents

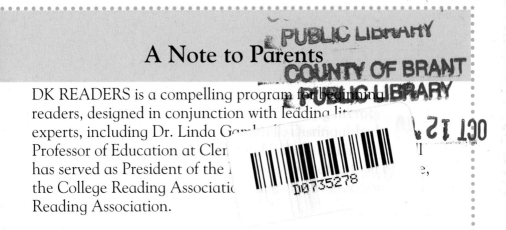

DK READERS is a compelling program for beginning readers, designed in conjunction with leading literacy experts, including Dr. Linda Gambrell, Professor of Education at Clemson University. Dr. Gambrell has served as President of the National Reading Conference, the College Reading Association, and the International Reading Association.

Beautiful illustrations and superb full-color photographs combine with engaging, easy-to-read stories to offer a fresh approach to each subject in the series. Each DK READER is guaranteed to capture a child's interest while developing his or her reading skills, general knowledge, and love of reading.

The five levels of DK READERS are aimed at different reading abilities, enabling you to choose the books that are exactly right for your child:

Pre-level 1: Learning to read
Level 1: Beginning to read
Level 2: Beginning to read alone
Level 3: Reading alone
Level 4: Proficient readers

The "normal" age at which a child begins to read can be anywhere from three to eight years old. Adult participation through the lower levels is very helpful for providing encouragement, discussing storylines, and sounding out unfamiliar words.

No matter which level you select, you can be sure that you are helping your child learn to read, then read to learn!

LONDON, NEW YORK, MUNICH,
MELBOURNE, and DELHI

Series Editor Deborah Lock
U.S. Editor Shannon Beatty
Designer Jemma Westing
Production Editor Sean Daly
Picture Researcher Rob Nunn
Jacket Designer Natalie Godwin

Reading Consultant
Linda Gambrell, Ph.D.

First American Edition, 2011
Published in the United States by
DK Publishing
375 Hudson Street, New York, New York 10014

11 12 13 14 15 10 9 8 7 6 5 4 3 2 1
001-182474-August 2011

Published in Great Britain by Dorling Kindersley Limited.
A catalog record for this book is available
from the Library of Congress.
ISBN: 978-0-7566-8923-0 (paperback)
ISBN: 978-0-7566-8924-7 (hardcover)

DK books are available at special discounts when purchased in bulk
for sales promotions, premiums, fund-raising, or educational use.
For details, contact:
DK Publishing Special Markets
375 Hudson Street, New York, New York 10014
SpecialSales@dk.com

Printed and bound in China by L Rex Printing Co., Ltd.

The publisher would like to thank the following for their kind
permission to reproduce their photographs:
a=above, b=below/bottom, c=center, l=left, r=right, t=top
Alamy Images: Arcticphoto 21br; blickwinkel / Linke 25br;
Rosemary Calvert 24bl; Frans Lanting Studio 22; Wayne Lynch / All
Canada Photos 30-31; William Sutton / Danita Delimont 1. **Corbis:**
Daisy Gilardini / Science Faction 2br, 20; Frans Lanting 27; Norbert
Wu / Science Faction 4. **FLPA:** Tui De Roy / Minden Pictures 5;
Norbert Wu / Minden Pictures 6. **Getty Images:** Digital Vision /
David Tipling 8-9; The Image Bank / Doug Allan 18; Photographer's
Choice / Sue Flood 3; Photographer's Choice RF / Martin Ruegner
11tl; Stone / Johnny Johnson 7br. **National Science Foundation,
USA:** 29tr. **naturepl.com:** 23br; Bryan and Cherry Alexander 29bl;
Suzi Eszterhas 32crb; Fred Olivier 2cr, 10, 12, 14-15, 16, 17br, 19;
Reinhard / ARCO 24-25. **NHPA / Photoshot:** A.N.T. Photo Library
13, 17tr, 32cla; Franco Banfi 7t; Rod Planck 32bl; John Shaw 23tr;
David Tipling 2tr, 9tr, 26; Woodfall / Steve Austin 21tr. **Science
Photo Library:** British Antarctic Survey 28; Art Wolfe 11b.
Jacket images: Front: Getty Images: Stone / Art Wolfe.
All other images © Dorling Kindersley
For further information see: www.dkimages.com

Discover more at
www.dk.com

Emperor Penguins

Written by Deborah Lock

DK Publishing

Brrr!

It is January, and the sun glints on the icy landscape of Antarctica. On the edges of the ice, Emperor penguins look out to sea.

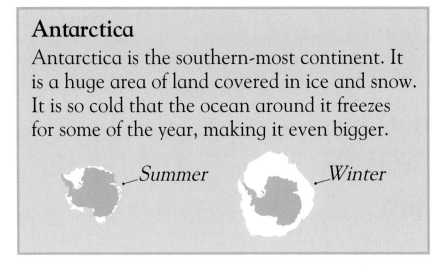

Antarctica

Antarctica is the southern-most continent. It is a huge area of land covered in ice and snow. It is so cold that the ocean around it freezes for some of the year, making it even bigger.

Summer   *Winter*

They are the tallest and heaviest of all penguins.
Their thick layers of shiny, waterproof feathers keep them warm and dry.

Slide! Splash!
Penguins are birds,
but they cannot fly.
Instead, they are great swimmers.
Their wings are flat and stiff
like flippers.
They dive in search of fish,
squid, and krill to eat.

Watch out!
Leopard seals lurk under
the edges of the ice
ready to ambush them.
With a speedy leap onto
the ice, the penguins
are safe again.

At the end of March, the penguins
begin their journey inland.
They are well fed since they will
not return to the ocean to eat
for a long time.
They waddle across the ice,
one after the other in a line.

Tobogganing

Penguins not only waddle, but they also slide across the ice, using their flippers and feet to push their bodies along.

They have a long way to go to get to their nesting area on the firm, thick ice.

Emperor penguins gather
together in colonies.
There could be more than
500,000 penguins
in each colony.
It is a noisy place to be
because they all sing
to each other.

A male penguin tries to impress
a female one with his voice.
If she is impressed, she will follow
the male around and stay with him.

In the middle of May, the mom
lays one large pear-shaped egg.
She is tired and hungry.
She shuffles close to the dad
and very carefully passes the egg
onto his feet.
The egg must not touch
the freezing ice.

He covers the egg with
his thick, warm layers
of feathers.
The mom starts
out again on
the long journey
back to the
icy ocean.

All is quiet at the colony.
It is June, which is wintertime
in Antarctica.
The temperature drops to below
-76°F (-60°C) and the icy winds
whip around the penguins.

The dads huddle together in
a large group to keep warm.
The ones on the outside shuffle
slowly around the edge.
They take turns to be in
the middle and on the outside.

For one month, there is total darkness. The sky is lit up with the colorful streaks of the Southern Lights.

Southern Lights

The Aurora Australis, or Southern Lights, is an amazing light show in the sky. The light is made by electrical particles from the Sun entering the Earth's atmosphere and colliding with the air.

Each dad balances his egg on top of his feet, keeping it warm. From time to time, the dad turns the egg very carefully, so that each part gets a chance to be the farthest away from the freezing ice.

It is August, and the sun begins
to shine for a few hours each day.
The young chicks start to hatch
out of their eggs.

They are hungry and call for food.
The dads have not eaten
for more than 100 days and
they are hungry, too.
When will the moms return?

After nine weeks away, the moms
appear at last.
During the winter, they have
eaten well and then traveled the
very long way back to the colony.

Dedicated parents

Adult penguins feed their chicks by bringing back up the food they swallow. Fish can be kept fresh in their stomachs for several days. Some parts of the food become a paste or a rich oil after a while.

Each dad passes his baby chick over to its mom.
He needs to be quick since the freezing ice will kill the chick within two minutes.
The chick can have a good meal at last from its mom.

The colony is a noisy place
once again.
The dads leave and it's now
the moms' turn to care for
their fluffy young chicks.

Dangers

The young chicks face many dangers. They could die from the cold or from hunger. They could also be attacked by Southern Giant Petrels.

As they get bigger, the chicks start to waddle around and huddle together for warmth. Then it's time for their moms to leave again to get more food. The chicks are left alone for the first time.

The dads return from
their journey to the ocean
and back.
But how will they each find
their own chick?

Squawk!

The colony is very noisy as
the hungry chicks call out
for their dads.
Each dad calls too and then
listens out for his own chick's call.
It may take hours wandering
among the thousands of chicks
for a dad to find his baby chick.

Piu! Piu!

The moms and dads shuttle back
and forth to the ocean for food
for themselves and their chicks.
As the sun shines longer each day,
the thin ice melts and the journey
to the ocean gets shorter
and shorter.
By November, the ocean is only
a short distance away from
the penguin colony.

Each new family can spend more time together.

The chicks are almost as big as their parents now.
Their gray, downy feathers begin to fall out and new shiny waterproof feathers form.
This is called molting.

Molting

During December, adult penguins also molt. They cannot swim until their new shiny waterproof feathers have grown.

Their moms and dads leave them for the last time to go and feed. The chicks will soon be ready to leave the colony, too.

An adult's waterproof feathers

It is January, and the sun shines
all day, everyday.
There is no darkness.
For the first time, the young
penguins shuffle across
the shiny ice sheets.

They head for the shimmering blue ocean.

They are hungry and eager for their first dip into the icy ocean to catch food for themselves.

Slide!

Splash!

Dive!

Penguin facts

There are 17 different types of penguin. They all live in the southern half of the world, but some prefer warmer climates than others. The most common types are African penguins that live on the southern coast of Africa and Humboldt penguins that live on the western coast of South America.

Adelie penguins are the smallest penguins that live in Antarctica. Their black and white colored markings make them look as if they are wearing tuxedos.

Chinstrap penguins live in Antarctica and on the Southern Islands nearby. They have a black band of feathers under their chin that looks like a strap.

Macaroni penguins live on the islands around Antarctica. They have colorful yellow feathers on top of their heads.